It is moderation that often brings health to Christians and churches. This book illustrates the dangers of two extremes—on one end of the spectrum is rigidity and on the other end there is chaotic permissiveness. Churches that are too rigid exert excessive control over the lives of their parishioners, stripping from them individual freedom; churches that are chaotically permissive offer no biblical boundaries for their parishioners, which can lead to out-of-control sinful behavior. Both rigidity and chaotic permissiveness can debilitate the lives and faith of parishioners. The book ends with a final summary that shows the importance of finding a healthy moderation in the center which emphasizes both individual liberty and biblical boundaries.

Rev. Dr. Lanny Law
Author of *God Knows Marriage Isn't Always Easy*

Judy De Wit is a clear and concise writer with years of experience in advocacy on behalf of the abused in the church. In this book she captures the essence of what spiritual abuse is—unbalanced leadership. It is leadership that is either lacking in the heart or lacking Christian standards. The healthy and spiritually rich church has both and is humble and transparent as well. This book is laden with great examples of healthy and unhealthy leadership behavior, which brings back memories of similar experiences in our own lives.

Rev. Ladan Jennings
Mill Creek Community Church (CRC)
Mill Creek, Washington

T0148467

Understanding Abusive Church Leadership

What It Looks Like and How It Debilitates the Life and Spirit of Church Members

Judy R. De Wit

iUniverse, Inc.
Bloomington

Understanding Abusive Church Leadership
What It Looks Like and How It Debilitates
the Life and Spirit of Church Members

iUniverse books may be ordered through booksellers or by contacting:

iUniverse
1663 Liberty Drive
Bloomington, IN 47403
www.iuniverse.com
1-800-Authors (1-800-288-4677)

ISBN: 978-1-4759-2674-3 (sc)
ISBN: 978-1-4759-2675-0 (e)
ISBN: 978-1-4759-2676-7 (dj)

Library of Congress Control Number: 2012908754

Printed in the United States of America

iUniverse rev. date: 6/18/2012

Contents

Acknowledgments

I wish to express my sincere appreciation to Rev. Harrison Newhouse, who provides me with encouragement and support when I get frustrated with the harmful ways in which the church responds to its people.

Thanks to Dr. Lanny Law, whose work with churches over many years has provided the support and encouragement I need to continue on with the subject of harmful and abusive leadership.

Thanks to Rev. Ladan Jennings, whose insight validates my continued work in this field.

With gratitude and love for God, I say thanks to Him for opening up my mind to understanding first how rigid and chaotic parenting approaches cause harm and abuse to families. From there He helped me to see that churches operate the way families do and gave me insight into how rigid and chaotic church leadership harms and abuses church members.

Judy R. De Wit

Note from the Author

I never thought of myself as smart enough to write a book. Yet, after ten years of studying books, taking classes, doing training, talking with experts, and researching materials on the topic of abuse in the church, I realized I had to put down on paper what I'd learned.

Breaking the Silence within the Church was written to help church leaders know how to identify, respond, and recover when abuse happens in their church. *Forgiving the Church* was written for anyone who is harmed or abused by the church and wants to begin the forgiveness process.

In Roman 13:10 it says, "Love does no harm." That should be true in our families, churches, and communities. But is it? *Understanding Abusive Church Leadership* and *How You Became You* challenge this question, for sadly, both church leaders and parents can abuse.

We are familiar with the different kinds of abuse. We know that sexual, physical, emotional, or any of the lesser abuses, can cause horrendous damage. Spiritual abuse is added when the abuse is committed by a church leader.

There are two kinds of spiritual abuse. One is rigid and controlling. A subtle (or sometimes not so subtle) and manipulative leader who misuses scripture and promotes the belief that our God is an angry God is engaging in spiritual abuse. This spiritual abuse is grounded in anxiety and is rooted in the idea that being a good Christian is about obeying all kinds of rules and laws. When members violate the church's rules and laws, messages from the church leaders are that the members are shameful human beings. Combine that with heavy doses of guilt and scriptural verses to support it, and abuse happens.

The second kind of spiritual abuse is when leadership is chaotic. A "whatever" attitude creates leaders doing whatever they believe is right in their own eyes and disregarding what is best for church members. Members also have the freedom to do what they want in both their personal and church lives when leadership lacks accountability, integrity, and honesty. Issues like having sex outside of marriage, drinking excessively and getting drunk, practicing homosexuality, and having abortions are not addressed by leadership. They as well as their members engage in lifestyles in which expectations and obedience to scripture are loosely regarded.

Both of these leadership approaches lack a healthy representation of God. God is neither an angry God nor a God who ignores sin. He is a God of justice and mercy. He calls His people to account when wrong happens and also extends mercy when He remembers the frailty and condition of His people.

What kind of spiritual leadership does your church use? Is it a rigid and self-righteous approach, or is it chaotic, using a "whatever" attitude? Hopefully, it is neither, and instead uses a healthy leadership approach that enhances and strengthens the faith and life of its members.

Judy R. De Wit

Introduction

Few church leaders know how to properly lead a church.

That thought may offend some of you, but I say this after having dealt with church leadership on all levels since the late 1990s. My engagement with church leaders is centered on situations where pastors and church leaders engaged in abuse and the system for addressing the allegations failed. More likely than not, I find church leaders struggling with what it means to demonstrate proper direction and leadership when crises arise. Sadly, when allegations of abuse have come forward, I've seen the response of church leaders add to the pain of victims instead of relieving it.

I am not trying to put the blame solely on the leaders. I understand that most pastors and elders do not have the training, experience, or education to know how to exhibit healthy leadership within a church. Many elders work in occupations that are very different from church administration. Younger pastors admit that they didn't learn enough in seminary about how to do all of the administrative parts of ministry. Some experienced pastors say they've had to learn it as the years went by, while others admit it's not their strong point in ministry work.

The local church is a unique institution. It has employees, volunteers, a budget, church members, policies and procedures, expectations, and a lot of opinions. It is a ministry, but it can look like a business. It doesn't make money, but it needs a lot of money to exist. No one person owns it, yet all of its members are invested in it. Sometimes changes are slow, while at other times its approach to issues and crises is fickle and reckless. Most who served in a leadership role in the church would admit: they would never run a business like how the church is run.

There are several challenging parts to serving as a church leader. However, I believe that the most important part is for church leaders to demonstrate that the church's reason for existence is to bring healing and restoration to God's broken world. The church should never be about harm and abuse. It should always be about compassion, love, and grace for all.

Sadly, however, the church fails in being what God mandated it to be. There are times, too many times, when the church neglects being an agent to healing and grace, and instead shows itself to be abusive. A rigid, harsh, angry, and controlling leadership approach creates church members' feelings of shame and guilt. Chaotic and reckless leadership styles bring confusion to their members and to an already hurting world.

Explore with me what abusive church leadership looks like and the harm it does. Grieve with me as you read about how people have turned away from God because of their experiences with the church. Let your anger surface when you think about how some churches portray God as an angry God, while others lead parishioners to believe God doesn't really care what happens. I encourage you to use your voice and to take a stand against any church whose leadership is abusive.

PART I
RIGID CHURCH LEADERSHIP

"do as we say." That meant that when the church leaders said something, everyone followed. Debate, discussion, or review of issues was not allowed. It was expected that members do whatever the leadership said, because they were the leaders and because they were appointed by God to serve as pastors and elders. Not only was it expected that the members would obey, but also that leadership was to be respected just because they were the leaders. And should any challenge be raised by a member, the issue and the member were quickly silenced.

The "do as we say" leadership style at the First Self-Righteous Church provided a long list of do's and don'ts for the church members. Women were never to teach a Bible study if a male was in attendance, jewelry and fine clothes were prohibited, and it was considered submissive if a woman endured abuse by an angry husband. Members were to keep strict Sunday observance. This meant that there was to be no buying or selling on Sundays, no weekly activities such as bike riding, using scissors, or watching television, and members were to attend both church services, no matter what the weather.

Church was hard, but so was home. Renee recalls many vicious fights with her brothers and her parents. Hitting, throwing things, bad language, and anger were common household events, and Renee tried to be the peacemaker in the midst of everything. Her mom drank too much, dad owned magazines that were inappropriate, and sneak-outs by her brothers were common. The conflict between what happened at church and what happened at home caused her to grow up feeling very confused about what was right and what was wrong.

That's what brought her to counseling. As tears flowed and anger surfaced, she realized that much of her depression was about the conflicting messages of her childhood. Now as an adult she couldn't sort it all out. It made no sense. How was she to act when the message from church said to do all the things the

Bible said, but her family showed hostile and harsh treatment toward one another? How was she to set and use boundaries with others when she saw her dad hiding bad magazines and then flirting with women in the community? How was she to respond appropriately to alcohol and drinking when the church outlawed any drinking and her mom had bottles of alcohol hidden throughout the house? Why were there two standards of how to live?

The First Self-Righteous Church had a significant role in Renee's confused thinking. Let's look closer at how the impact and influence of this kind of church can have a devastating effect on someone like Renee—and maybe you.

Chapter 2
Rigid and Spiritually Abusive Churches

*He replied, "Isaiah was right when he prophesied about you
hypocrites; as it is written:*

*'These people honor me with their lips,
but their hearts are far from me.
They worship me in vain;
their teachings are but rules taught by men.'* ·

*You have let go of the commands of God and are holding on
to the traditions of men."*
Matthew 7:6–8

What is spiritual abuse?

Spiritual abuse is when a pastor or other church leader uses
his/her power to control and manipulate their church members
while using literal interpretations of scripture to support their
demands. The misrepresentation of God is also spiritually
abusive.

Judy R. De Wit

What does spiritual abuse look like in the rigid and controlling church?

Rigid and controlling leadership is made up of leaders driven by fear. Believing that God is an angry God, rigid and controlling leaders are anxious because they fear their members will do things that make God angry. Wanting to avoid ticking God off, rigid and controlling leaders find ways to control their members. They control their members by making a long list of rules and laws and requiring their members to obey them. By doing this, it is the leaders' hope that God will be good to them.

Driven by that anxiety, they use a literal interpretation of the Bible. By taking scriptural verses out of context, they are able to manipulate the Bible to make it say what they want it to say. When they use this approach, their position of power increases, because now it looks like the Bible backs them up in their efforts to control and lead. They take a verse like "Sarah, who obeyed Abraham and called him her master" (1 Peter 3:6,) and use it to give leaders permission to be harsh with other women and their own wives. Or the verse "Rejoice that you participate in the sufferings of Christ" (1 Peter 4:13,) is used to shut down any sad or angry feelings about things that happen in members' lives. They are to rejoice instead. Both of these are twisted interpretations of scripture, which cause leadership to have more power. This is spiritually abusive.

Drawing from these scriptural interpretations, rigid and controlling church leaders devise many rules and laws, which they expect their members to obey. Rules about dress, swearing, lying, cheating, Sunday observance, and money are obvious. Rules about sex, adultery, drinking, abuse, and assaults are unspoken. It is expected that members know both kinds of rules.

Spiritual abuse happens when church leaders falsely portray who God is and what He wants His Church to be. This misrepresentation of God causes members to think that the way their leaders conduct themselves is representative of how God is. So if their leaders become angry and punitive when members make mistakes, they learn to believe that God is like that too. This creates an unhealthy and wrong view of who God is, neglecting the truth that God is also a God of grace and mercy.

Therefore, rigid and controlling church leaders spiritually abuse their members in two main ways. They control their members by expecting their members to obey their many laws and rules. Secondly, they spiritually abuse their members when they misrepresent God by using anger, rigidity, and harshness in their leadership approach.

Church leaders spiritually abuse by using rigidity

There are several ways that rigid and controlling leaders maintain their control over their people. They use the following:

- shame
- guilt
- rigid boundaries
- appearances
- conditional love
- the church knows best
- chosen people
- don't feel
- traditions
- acceptance and approval
- entitlement

Let's look at each one more closely.

Judy R. De Wit

Shame

First, there is shame. Shame messages from leadership tell people that they are defective, they don't measure up, and they're not good enough. Shame says that the person is bad and that he/she won't amount to anything. Shame messages get at the personhood of someone and attacks self-worth, self-esteem, and value. Van Vonderen (1989, p. 41) defines shame as messages given to family members that they are defective and inadequate. He says that over time, these messages become ingrained into the family member and drives that person to find ways to prove he/she is good enough. This can happen in families and also in churches.

Shame is used when a church leader tells members that because they drink, they can no longer come to worship. Shame happens when a congregant is told that having a child out of wedlock means exclusion from the fellowship. It is spiritually abusive to use shame as a way to control church members.

Guilt

Guilt is used to control church members. Guilt from leadership is messages that church members are bad because of what they are or are not doing. Guilt is used to control, as when a parent says that their son won't be allowed to take over the family business because he goes to the wrong church. Control by guilt happens when a church leader tells a congregant that because he/she doesn't help out often enough at church activities, there's to be no participation in a small group. It is control by guilt if the church leader says that a member hasn't helped out enough with the care of an aging parent or the member's giving to the church is not enough. This is spiritually abusive.

Rigid boundaries

In the rigid church, there are rigid boundaries. This kind of boundary says that a church leader or member will step over the line in disciplining another person because they believe the person needs to be corrected. Rigid boundaries come with narrow expectations about the way things are supposed to be. This means that when a violation occurs, the rigid church leader uses his/her rigid boundaries to come after the person and chastise him or her. The church leader's feeling of entitlement to "tell someone off" comes from the belief that church leaders have special rights. Rigid people are the "know-it-alls." This approach does not respect the rights of others and is spiritually abusive.

Laaser (2004, pp. 94–95) speaks about rigidity in families. He defines family abuse as using rigid boundaries in such a way that affirming, loving, and encouraging children is withheld. This leads to emotional abandonment. This idea can also be applied to the leadership of a church family.

Appearances

Appearances are used by church leaders to control. Within a rigid and controlling church, there is a certain way to look and be. It's expected that members will act, look, and speak a certain way within the church and the community. If there isn't compliance with that expectation, church leaders will sometimes subtly and sometimes openly pressure the member to make changes. When skirts are too short, when hair is not appropriate, or when a member exhibits an "inappropriate" attitude, church leaders and others will either shun the member back to obedience or they will confront the wrongdoer until compliance is shown. Appearance is important for this kind of faith community. This is spiritually abusive.

Conditional love

Conditional love is used in spiritually abusive churches. Conditional love is love shown to others based on what they do. Church members only receive love and acceptance from leadership when they obey the rules, follow the leaders of the church, and do what they are told. Conditional love is based on conditions. Love is withheld when someone messes up. Praise and affirmation are awarded when a person carries through on what is to be done. Love is not free; it is earned.

The church knows best

Spiritually abusive church leaders tell members how to think and what to do. Should anyone present a point of view that is not in compliance with the leaders' approach or the church's teaching, church leaders are quick to correct that wrong thinking and bring the member back to where the church stands on the issue. Should a member be doing something that shows a contradiction to a stand the church takes, leaders quickly summon the member and tell the person to stop, for there is only one way to do things and that is the way the church has done it for years. There is neither time nor room to discuss issues or share other viewpoints. Outsiders may view this micromanaging as intrusive and invasive, but for members, it is viewed as "the church knows best."

Chosen people

Spiritually abusive churches convince their members that they are the only ones who are saved. Using 1 Peter 2:9, "But you are a chosen people, a royal priesthood," they convince their members that they are the only ones who are going to heaven. All other churches are wrong. Their church is the only right church. This controlling approach prevents its members from leaving the church because they'll go to hell if they do.

Don't feel

Spiritually abusive churches have little time for feelings. They believe that members should not devote time to feeling the harm or hurt that comes into their lives. There is little time for grieving the loss of a loved one, for feeling sad when a marriage breaks up, or for feeling upset when there is a wayward child. Anger and fears are to be ignored and denied, for life is too short to be fussing with feelings. Along with this is the fear of having feelings. Rigid leaders and members shut down their own feelings when they surface because it makes them feel weak. Being vulnerable may lead to an experience that is unknown to them. That would be scary and is therefore avoided.

Laaser (2004, p. 97) says family abuse happens when "a person is not allowed to have his or her feelings." He calls this a kind of "mind rape" and says that when churches engage in this behavior with their members, it becomes "religious mind rape." He stresses the importance of allowing feelings to be felt so that people's emotional stages, such as grieving the loss of a loved one, can happen.

Traditions

"This is the way it's always been done" is what spiritually abusive churches say. What they fear is change. Change does not comply with how their forefathers did things and change may break the rules. Breaking the rules is bad. Doing things differently is bad. Fears of change are grounded in the possibility that leadership will lose control and then what will happen to the church? Spiritually abusive leadership fears change.

Acceptance and approval issues

Everyone wants to be accepted and liked by others. In the rigid and controlling church, acceptance from leadership and pew members is paramount to living in the faith community.

Approval from others within the church and getting the acceptance from fellow members is the lifeline for survival in the rigid church. Members are devastated if they are shunned by the fellowship or are excluded in some way. For them, isolation and alienation from the church community is nearly impossible to bear. This is spiritually abusive.

Entitlement

Rigid and controlling church leaders feel they are entitled, or have "rights," to treat members as they wish. They believe they are special. They believe they are given power that has little to no accountability or responsibility. They believe they can do things to their members because they are entitled to it. This entitlement allows them to fire church personnel without reason, to say and do things that are harsh, unreasonable, and demeaning, and to use anger to accomplish what they want.

Church leaders spiritually abuse by misrepresenting God

Pastors and church leaders represent God. Their behavior, attitude, and treatment of others should reflect the love of God. However, when leaders show anger, hostility, unfairness, control, and abuse to others, they misrepresent God and people come to believe that God is like that. God is misrepresented and spiritual abuse happens when emotional, verbal, physical, or sexual abuse happens. Victims of abuse come to believe that they are bad because someone who stands for God did bad things to them. God is angry and they deserved it because they are bad.

Spiritual abuse happens when executive church board members entitle themselves to fire a lead director without good reason. It is spiritually abusive when an elder entitles himself to pound his fist on the council table and demands that things go his way. This is also emotionally abusive. Spiritual abuse happens when a pastor is angry at a church member and entitles himself to tell the person that he is going to hell if he doesn't change. Sexual, physical, emotional, and spiritual abuse happens when a church leader entitles himself to touch a woman who is not his wife inappropriately.

Conclusion

Spiritually abusive church leaders use control and manipulation to get their members to meet their demands. The members obey the abusive leaders because they fear what could happen if they don't. Abusive church leaders also entitle themselves to treat their members as they see fit and abuse their positions and power by misrepresenting God.

Chapter 3
The Effects of Rigid and Spiritually Abusive Churches

On the outside you appear to people as righteous
but on the inside you are full of hypocrisy and wickedness.
Matt. 23:28

Pride

Pride is the heart of the problem at the First Self-Righteous Church, and its leaders suffer from big doses of it. Their pride manifests itself in how well they dictate to the members what they are supposed to do, how well they know scripture and can recite verses when needed, and how they are dedicated to maintaining the church as it always has been. The cycle of spiritual abuse, from generation to generation, stays intact because of the way it's always been done has never been broken.

But the leaders aren't the only ones who suffer from pride. So do their members. When a church requires its members to follow a lot of rules and the members believe they follow them well, thoughts of how good they are take root. Pride takes root. And the members keep score. The members of the First Self-Righteous Church can tell you who worked last on a church committee, who served food at the last fellowship supper, and who gave extra money to a needy cause. They know who has a lower score than they do, who commits greater sins than they do, and what the pecking order is for each member seated in the pews. As their pride grows and flourishes on the inside, members maintain somber and sober faces on the outside. They appear righteous, but their hearts are "full of hypocrisy and wickedness" (Matt. 23:28) and pride.

Pride is about insecurity. The insecurity of the members of the First Self-Righteous Church is layered with much anxiety. Anxiousness and fears abound as pressure to be a certain way dominates their approach to faith and life. Their anxiety and fears drive them to try harder, pray more, work extra, and be more obedient.

How rigid leadership spiritually affects church members

Spiritual abuse shows itself in many different ways for the members of the First Self-Righteous Church. Sadly, the overall results of a rigid approach to leadership are that the faith and life of the church's members are debilitated. Disempowered, the members believe that God is about guilt and their faith is about fear.

The effects of rigid church leadership include the following:

- perfectionism
- shame
- guilt
- rigid boundaries
- defensiveness and reactivity
- rebellion or overcompliance
- identity defined by the church

- spiritual abuse

Let's look at each more closely.

Perfectionism

First, there is perfectionism. Perfectionist church members strive to do things perfectly because they fear they may make a mistake. They check and recheck to make sure things are perfect. They check in with themselves to make sure they are on track with what the church wants. They check in with others to see how they are doing. Their relationships are measured by how much they are serving others; they do not expect anything from anyone, and put themselves last on the totem pole. Self-care is a selfish thing and others' needs always come before their own. Whether it's in relationships, jobs, or appearances, much time and energy are put into being and looking perfect. Their perfectionism is driven by the anxiety that they not make mistakes.

Shame

Spiritually abused church members feel great shame. A person who lives with heavy doses of shame is easily controlled by the church because shame eats at the core of who they are. They submit to the authority of the church because of their poor self-esteems and self-concepts, and their low sense of worth prevents them from asserting themselves and expressing their thoughts and opinions. Controlling and manipulating church members are easy when church leaders use shame.

Guilt

When a church shames, its members feel guilt. Their guilt drives them to do things because they think they have to in order to be good enough. They volunteer to do many extra things in the church, believe that the more they do the better person they are, and don't assert themselves when they should because they do not feel worthy or good enough to do so.

Members of a spiritually abusive church are easily threatened and intimidated because of this guilt. They are taught that if they speak up, they are being insubordinate to church authority, and such behavior could lead to church discipline. The thought of facing church discipline makes them fear not being liked. If that happened, the church community would come to hear about their sin and they would be ostracized and shunned by the faith community. They are driven by guilt.

Rigid boundaries

Abused church members believe there is only one way to do things: the way the church tells them to. They shut down the emotions of others, cut off their own emotions, and use Bible verses about being strong and courageous. This is what Laaser (2004) describes as emotional abandonment.

Defensiveness and reactivity

Criticism runs high in the spiritually abusive church. This causes members to be defensive and reactive when something does not go right. Their defensiveness and reactivity stems from years of being criticized by family and the church. They are exhausted from being undermined and belittled and it shows in the way they react to those around them.

Rebellion and overcompliance

There is rebellion and overcompliance in the spiritually abusive church. Rebellion can show itself in several ways. There is the refusal to listen to church authority, refusal to obey the rules of the church, excessive drinking and drug use, promiscuity, violence and more. These behaviors are responses to living in a rigid and controlling environment. This rebellion is about church

what drives them to spend so much time in Bible study and prayer. For others, there is little to no interest in studying the Bible or praying because God is so distant anyway. They reason that it's a waste of time to read the Bible and pray to a God who is uninterested.

Spiritually abusive churches focus on thinking and doing, but have no time for feeling. The list of do's and don'ts is long, but no time is to be spent on feeling. Feelings are silly and fickle and work doesn't get done if members feel too much. Crying is to be done in private. Don't talk about faith or what God has done in one's life. Members are to know God and do what He says, but He's not to be experienced.

Faith is debilitated in a spiritually abusive church when its members attend church out of duty and routine. They show up for worship because that is expected. They give money to the poor because the church says so. They serve on a church committee because they're told to. They read the Bible because the pastor says to. This approach makes church members feel empty and discouraged, for life and God seem pointless.

Conclusion

Pride is the heart of the problem in spiritually abusive churches. Pride is about the fears, insecurities, and anxieties of both church leadership and its members. Perfectionism, shame, intimidation, criticism, rebellion, and identity issues occur because of this. The faith of the members is debilitated and their spiritual growth is stunted when spiritual abuse happens. Church, faith, and life become routine and empty.

Chapter 4
Stories of Rigid and Spiritually Abusive Churches

A horrible and shocking thing has happened in the land:
The prophets prophesy lies, the priests rule by their own
authority,
And my people love it this way.

Jer. 5:30–31

1. It was a small rural town that took great pride in its churches and community. One of the town's churches in particular was drawn to an ultra-conservative approach to worship and life, and its members were driven to perform as their church leaders expected. Determined to show others they measured up to the demands of their church, the members of this church attended all church meetings and Bible studies, sent their children to the Christian school, were diligent about personal and family devotions, and focused on memorizing scripture. The church leaders were proud of how their people submitted to their authority, and secretly they were pleased

with how easy it was to control and manipulate their members. However, church leadership was not what it appeared to be, or what members or outsiders would expect.

Soon allegations of sexual abuse came forward by several women of the community. When it became known to the council of the church, the leaders were confused about what to do. Some protected the pastor and said he would never do such a thing. They called the victims liars. Some were neutral, unable to discern what the truth was and therefore unable to determine how to address the allegations. A few knew that protecting the pastor and remaining neutral were the wrong stands to take, and yet, they were too intimidated to speak up and confront the pastor.

Soon a few of the members asked to meet with the council to discuss what was happening. When they confronted the elders and shared their concerns, some of the leaders were quick to silence the issues raised. Quoting from scripture, the elders told the church members they were to submit to the authority of the church and that church leaders knew best how to lead the church.

Anger increased as more of what happened was disclosed to the public. Refusing to be easily swayed, the two sides took matters into their own hands and the fight was on. Going to the grocery store, meeting each other in the fellowship hall, and inappropriate phone calls to the other side created divisions and disharmony in the church. What appeared to be a church that prided itself in its members obeying all the rules and expectations now became a place of harm and destruction. Leadership was ill equipped to know how to manage their people. The once easy scripture quotes that silenced any problem were useless and disregarded. For once, the members of the church were determined to search out and seek out the truth about what was happening, and simplistic answers from leadership didn't cut it.

The rigid, self-righteous approach to leadership and church membership came to an end. No longer were scripture quotes used, the insistence that rules and laws be obeyed diminished, the anxiety to perform and be perfect fell away, and the threats by leadership to submit to their authority was ended. Members were exhausted from the pretending they had done for years.

Spiritual abuse happened when the pastor misrepresented the Church of Christ by sexually abusing women. The pastor is to bring healing and recovery to the people of his congregation, not harm. His behavior was also sexually, physically, and emotionally abusive.

Spiritual abuse also happened when the leadership used scripture to protect themselves as leaders and when the leaders were rigid and controlling toward their members. Falsehood and pretending dominated. Their approach created anxiety, perfectionism, and fears, preventing healthy spiritual growth and maturity.

2. The board of the church was not satisfied with the work of one of their directors. As time passed, a performance review of the director occurred, and there was a discussion of areas where the director's

performance in some of the day-to-day demands of his work was lacking.

Others who worked with him were engaged with him and found him supportive and helpful. He was open to new ideas about how to resolve problems and was solid in his commitment to Christ and the church.

A meeting was called and his board told him to resign from his position with no prior notice. He complied and resigned although there were no allegations of moral failure and no complaints of impropriety. He left feeling confused and hurt about why this happened.

His church had many unanswered questions as the events of the resignation became known. No clear reason was given from the board for forcing his resignation. As time passed, more questions surfaced without good answers. It appeared that the board became rigid and controlling and wanted things to go their way.

The director left feeling spiritually abused by the church. The lack of respect and dignity with which they approached his resignation created the director's own disillusionment about what the church really was. Shame dominated for the director and his family because the board failed to follow a due process that ensured dignity for the leader as well as respect for the work he did. Although church members made several efforts to get an explanation about what happened, nothing more was done.

3. She worked as a director in one of the offices of the church's regional denominational buildings. Her approach included a long list of rules that she believed both the church leaders and members should follow. When things didn't go her way, she displayed her disapproval through anger fits, including cutting people off from dialogue with her, telling others off, and clearly labeling each person she dealt with as "in her camp" or "not in her camp."

When complaints about her punitive and retaliatory approach came to her supervisor and governing board, the leaders were fearful of addressing and handling the issue. The leaders' own fears of the director's anger caused a lack of accountability on behalf of the leaders, which increased her power in that position. As she began to realize the fear that her supervisors had toward her, she took advantage of it and increased her demands. Her rigidity and control showed itself in a variety of ways. She believed she was entitled to share private and confidential information of one of her call-ins with a pastor in a different region, without proper permission. When it was brought to her governing board, it was called "pastoral care." She took it upon herself to see that a certain pastor was defrocked from ministry, although the governing mandate for her work did not allow such action. She lied to the president of her governing board when he confronted her about her conduct. When the truth was established, she lied to the board president and nothing else was done.

As time passed, she managed to develop a system where there were only certain people that she was willing to work with. These individuals, who followed her every expectation, were privileged recipients of her office's services. Others, who had good ideas about how to address the issues her office was responsible for, were ignored and even defamed by her. Her office became all about her and those who were in "her camp."

Her approach was spiritually abusive because she used the power of her position to get what she wanted. She showed favoritism toward those who supported her and diminished others who didn't. Her anger was a misrepresentation of God.

4. People of his congregation were easily swayed by his approach as pastor of their church. He had a way of taking command and dictating how programs, committees, and worship should be. This made things easy for the council, for now their workload was reduced. They simply let the pastor take control of things and it seemed that everyone was happy.

During worship, he directed the worship leaders in what songs to sing and how they were to be sung. When someone else led the congregation in prayer, he made sure the leader wrote out the prayer prior to the service so that he could approve of what it said. He directed the deacons as to how they were to distribute money to the poor of the community, and when there were requests for support from new nonprofit agencies, he made sure he gave his personal approval prior to presenting it to council.

His intrusive approach included involving himself in committee work that was outside his domain. Convinced he was an authority in all areas of church work, he entitled himself to write a long letter to a regional leader, accusing her of doing things she never did. In that letter, he threatened the chairperson that if she didn't comply with his demands, he would do something to her. When the chairperson presented a copy of his letter to the council, they covered it up and did nothing about it.

He became more and more demanding and controlling as he became more concerned about his appearance and performance. His rigidity caused medical issues for him, including high blood pressure and sleepless nights. As he ruminated about all of the things he needed to do to ensure things were perfect, his ability to preach slowly began to diminish and his anxiety took over. It was as if he could not breathe.

His congregation became exhausted from his micromanaging, and they began to withdraw from committee work and leadership because of the high expectations of the pastor. A few recognized what was going wrong while most began to believe they just weren't good enough to participate in church functions.

Then what took place was the opposite of what most would expect. It was discovered that he was drinking excessively. He admitted he was addicted to prescription medication. He said that much of his time was spent going from doctor to doctor to keep his addiction going. He knew it was wrong, but he was unable to stop.

The pastor spiritually abused the congregants in his controlling approach to his church members and the faith community. He spiritually abused the members of his church by misrepresenting himself in his work for the church.

5. He was diligent in his work as pastor. He had a pleasing personality, was charming, and was easily accepted and loved by his congregation. His conservative approach to worship and interpretation of the Bible seemed to fit the needs of the congregation. He preached with eloquence, and in Bible studies he demonstrated good Bible knowledge.

But things changed as time passed. Certain issues were raised by the elder board as well as by certain members. It seemed that the pastor was not working the expected office hours and the regional body of churches expressed concerns about work not being completed when needed. When the elders confronted the pastor about not getting things done, his reasons for the lapse seemed acceptable.

But then more problems and complaints surfaced.

The pastor's sermon preparation and council work were poorly done. The elders sensed that the sermons lacked content and they were becoming weary of the delays regarding council directives for the pastor. When asked again about his time management, the pastor expressed that things were getting done, that the workload was too much for him, and that he was doing the best he could.

Then it happened. A council member decided to review the pastor's computer when the pastor was out of the office and found that porn sites were frequently viewed by the pastor. When the elder board confronted him, the pastor admitted he was preoccupied with pornography and devoted much of his time to viewing it. He admitted that he had started back in his college days, and said that he needed a reward when stressed out and viewing porn met his emotional needs.

The pastor had two sides to himself. He showed his conservative side when it came to God, the church, and the Bible, and he had a dark side that was his sexual addiction. Spiritual abuse happened when he misrepresented God and His church.

6. The youth director hired to help out with the church's youth program came with good recommendations. He showed himself to have a good understanding of the Bible and was especially gifted in interacting with young teens about their spiritual lives and needs.

    As time passed, some of the young women in the youth group noticed he gave more attention to certain members of the youth group than others. Most of those getting the attention were considered the popular girls of the group. He gave them rides home when it wasn't needed, he met with these girls at restaurants, and when the youth group needed volunteers, they were the first people he asked to help.

    Soon it became much more than that. The girls were spending time at his house watching movies, his conversations with them were more private in nature, and there were times he obviously was looking at them during meetings and youth activities.

He denied doing any of these things when confronted by the senior pastor. He said that he, as always, had concerns about all of the youth of the church. He claimed that the interactions with certain young women were appropriate and some of the youth members must be jealous.

Later a complaint came forward, alleging that the youth director had been seen kissing two of the young women in the youth group. When confronted, he admitted that it was true.

He misrepresented God and the church by becoming too emotionally involved with certain young women from the group. He spiritually abused the young women, the youth group, and all those involved. He created an unsafe environment for the members of the youth group and abused the power of his position by using it to meet his emotional needs.

7. He was rigid and controlling. He was one of the lead directors of his denomination, and his staff soon came to realize his demanding and harsh approach. His temper could flare easily, and if something wasn't done right, his staff feared the repercussions of their mistakes. Although he and they were working for the church, somehow respect for one another and the concept of being a team together for the greater good never applied to the director's treatment of his staff.

There was a time when a victim of their church system came forward to present allegations of child sexual abuse. When all that could be done was done, the director became irritated with the victim. During the last visit to his office, the director basically kicked the victim out of his office, telling him his case was closed and it was never to be talked about again. Tearful and hurt, the victim shared what had happened in the director's office with his advocate that evening. The victim died the next day.

Three weeks later, the advocate confronted the director about what had taken place between him and the victim. Again, the director became irritated about things and told the advocate he was hanging up the phone.

The director's harsh and noncaring approach spiritually reabused and revictimized the victim. He was also emotionally abusive to the victim and those he worked with. His misrepresentation of God to others was emotionally abusive.

PART II
CHAOTIC CHURCH LEADERSHIP

Chapter 5
At the Community Church of Chaos

Do not be wise in your own eyes.

Prov. 3:7

Joy came to counseling because she started to feel depressed and anxious after her husband and she began attending a new church. She said she liked her new church although it was very different from her growing up church. The more they attended and became involved with the church, the more old memories were surfacing. She found herself frequently comparing the two churches. The more she thought about the churches, the more panicky she became. She was nervous and scared during church time although she described the people friendly and found the pastor was kind and sincere. She liked how they did worship. Yet, something wasn't right and she wanted to understand why.

When asked what she remembered about her childhood church, she called it the Community Church of Chaos. One of the first things that came to mind was how the pastor of the church was unpredictable. By that she meant that sometimes the pastor did things she didn't expect. He would make smart remarks and wise cracks during the service. He would tell unusual jokes and stories. The response from the people was uncertain. Sometimes they would laugh and sometimes they wouldn't. It seemed that some were embarrassed. Her parents never gave clear answers when she would ask them about what those stories or comments meant. As a child, she wondered whether the stories he told were from the Bible or not.

She remembers about a time when the pastor told one of the older members to sit closer to the front of church. The pastor told the man that he was tired of seeing him sit in the same bench week after week. Church became awkwardly silent. Then the man got up and left.

She remembers more about the pastor. She once saw him kiss a woman of the congregation. It happened when she went downstairs to bring something to the kitchen. When she came around the corner, there he was, kissing a woman. Not sure what she should do, she quietly turned around and left.

She overheard a conversation between her parents a short time later. They seemed to be concerned about something that Mom heard at the grocery store. Mom was talking about how someone complained to the elders of the church that the pastor touched someone inappropriately. She wasn't able to hear much of the details, but the more she thought about it the more anxious she became. She started to wonder if she should tell them what she saw in the church basement.

She began to remember more about what happened at the Community Church of Chaos as counseling continued. The leadership was called the elder board. There were about eight or nine of them. She could recall several of them by name and wondered why these men served as leaders of the church.

One of them was divorced two times. His third wife was her aunt and she recalled many discussions by her parents when

Mom's sister dated and then married this man. It was something about how marrying someone who was previously divorced two times was bad. There was another man who served as an elder who had two children from two different women. As a child, Joy felt confused about how that worked. This man also lived with a woman he wasn't married to. Another elder of the church, who she remembers as big and husky and with a deep voice, was scary to her. She remembers reading in the local paper about the time he was arrested for hitting his wife. He went to jail.

There were other things that were confusing about this church. The elders would drink and gamble. It was something known as "the elders night out." This meant that some of them would travel to a large city, about an hour away, and they would drink at a bar and gamble. There was talk about how some lost money, some made money, and some became very drunk. Who was the designated driver was the butt of the jokes. She remembers the elders talking about bad pictures and there was a time she saw them exchange bad magazines while talking after church on the parking lot.

In tears, she told more. It was about the songs that were sung during worship, the lack of attention for the children, and the inconsistencies she saw between what the Bible said and what the church people did. Again and again she said, "This church was so chaotic and confusing. I can't sort through what I am remembering. Everyone did as they wanted."

another, that is okay. "Wounds from a friend can be trusted" (Prov. 27:6) is done without respect for one another and without love. Each defines love according to what that person thinks it is. It's spiritually abusive when the concept of love is used to treat people as one wishes.

Fortune (1995, p. 48-49) speaks about love and lust in this way. She says that "'Lust' is the urge to possess or dominate sexually" (p. 48). She shares that lust is about having power over another person and that lust needs to be controlled when sexual feelings surface for another. Love, she shares, is not about harm. It is about sincere concern for the well-being of another.

Each knows best

Each decides in one's own heart what is right and good because there are no rules. Each knows best what should be done when there are problems. Putting the law into their own hands, members of the chaotic church do as they wish because there are no standards or guidelines to abide by. What is good and right for one may not be good or right for another. Each knows best what needs to be done and there is no accountability or discussion about the decisions made. Spiritual abuse happens when church leaders and members go their way to resolve issues and problem.

Everyone is saved

Everyone is saved in the Community Church of Chaos. God is understood as being a loving and gracious God. He is all good. Everyone is going to heaven. Know that going to heaven is a sure thing if one's name is written in the membership directory. There is little concern about how the members live their lives when "my name is written in the book of Life." Enjoy life, do what one wants, because everyone is saved and going to heaven. This wrong concept of salvation is spiritually abusive.

Judy R. De Wit

If it feels good, do it

Do not deprive oneself of anything that God gives to enjoy. He made "the earth and everything in it" so chaotic members want to ensure that all of it is enjoyed. The chaotic church believes members can do things if it feels good, such as drinking till one gets drunk or flirting with the opposite sex.

No traditions

There are no traditions at the Community Church of Chaos. Traditions would limit and prevent the important part of self-expression and spontaneity. It would limit people from doing what they want to do. Therefore, it is best not to have something like traditions and routines at the church. It's spiritually abusive when order for worship and life are not well-established by the church for both leaders and members.

No accountability

Anyone who breaks the rules is subject to the ones who made them. When a child is disobedient to her teacher, she must answer to her teacher. A citizen, who breaks a speeding law, answers to the officer who stopped him. However, when there are no rules in a church, there is no one to answer to. The chaotic church likes it this way.

Individualism

This kind of church believes in the approach of "do as you want." With this, there are no others that people can take their problems to, because there is no chain of command. People who are hurt by church leaders are left to resolve it on their own because there is no accountability of church leaders to other church leaders. This happens because of the lack of rules, guidelines, and accountability. This individualism approach may seem attractive at first since it allows freedom from being

48

confronted by anyone. However, a closer look at no structure creates an institution that has no protection.

Church leaders spiritually abuse by misrepresenting God

Pastors and church leaders misrepresent God when they use chaotic leadership. This means that the way they lead shows how God is: no accountability, no show of responsibility, and no rules and guidelines to live by. Members of the chaotic church come to believe that the way their leaders do things is also the way God does things. Therefore, they have no fear of breaking rules with God because if their leaders don't care what they do, God apparently doesn't care either.

When allegations of sexual abuse come forward against a pastor, the elders of the chaotic church have no response. They don't respond to it because they know that people do that kind of thing, it's not their problem, and she should have known better than to be fooling around with the pastor. When children are getting hurt in youth programs at the chaotic church, the church leaders are quick to dismiss themselves from the issues. They believe that parents are the ones who should do something about it, not them. The elders choose not to be involved in the problem when the pastor becomes involved in pornography on the church computer. They refuse to hold the pastor accountable.

Conclusion

The Community Church of Chaos is a community that has no rules. There is no fear of accountability or confrontation when there are no rules or guidelines to follow. One can do as one wants. God is kind and merciful and everyone is going to heaven. Church leaders do not tell their members what they can and cannot do and when problems arise, it's "to each his own" in how it is to be resolved. Boundaries are nonexistent and "if it feels good, do it."

Chapter 7
The Effects of Chaotic and
Spiritually Abusive Churches

The wicked bring shame and disgrace.

Pr. 13:5

Identity

Identity issues are the heart of the problem at the Community Church of Chaos. Leaders and their members do not know who they are because there are no expectations or accountability that sets out a structure that defines them. Therefore, the members of this church struggle with who they are and what they are capable of being simply because there are no expectations or accountability.

Members of this church are confused. There is no one in charge, no one to enforce rules or expectations, and their understanding of who God is and what He is about is vague and distorted. God is made out to be something different for each member. What one member may read and interpret about God from the

Bible can be quite different from what another member may believe.

Creeds and confession for the church are nonexistent. It would be wrong for a church to dictate what a group as a whole would teach and believe in regard to God. The chaotic church accepts a large gamut of ideas and beliefs about God, faith, and life, for it's impossible to determine who is right or wrong about such matters. As members struggle with knowing who they are, they also struggle with knowing who God is.

There are also issues of codependency. This means that they find their identity in other people. What others think becomes what they think. They do what others do. They want to belong to the church so they become a print of what others are. They think and believe like their leaders and others do. They don't think for themselves.

How chaotic leadership spiritually affects church members

The effects of chaotic church leaders include the following:

- shame
- inappropriate guilt
- poor boundaries
- appearances
- conditional love
- each knows best
- everyone is saved
- no traditions
- no accountability
- individualism
- spiritual abuse

Let's look at each one more closely.

Shame

Shame happens when a church leader says to a member who is abused by the church, "Just get over it and move on." The church shames when church leaders call others bad names and treat others with harshness. Shame happens when some members are treated differently than others. Bad shame is bad because it goes after the personhood of a person. It attacks the "who" of the person, not what the person does. This is spiritually abusive.

Inappropriate guilt

Members of a chaotic church have little guilt. They don't feel bad when they mistreat someone because they were not taught to respect one another. Shame is not felt when they offend someone, therefore, no guilt is present either.

Poor boundaries

Poor boundaries happen in chaotic churches. Chaotic church leaders use poor boundaries when they involve themselves in the matter of others that are not their business. Poor boundaries are seen in churches when church leaders tell parents how to parent, when church leaders are having sex with those who are not their spouse, and when personal and private information of members and others are spoken freely to those who do not need to know. This is spiritually abusive.

Appearances

Things are reckless in the chaotic church. Disregard for privacy and lack of respect for one another is rampant. This includes appearances. It doesn't matter how one appears or how things are done in a chaotic church. Getting drunk, having an affair, breaking up marriages, and hurting children happen because of their own disrespect for self. It's almost as if they are shameless.

They do shameful and shameless things because there is no respect for self or others.

Shamelessness is seen in words and behavior. A leader's shameless comment can be, "It will be good when that old lady dies. Then she won't be bothering us anymore." Or "Everyone does porn, don't you know that? Don't worry, God doesn't mind."

Conditional love

There is conditional love and unconditional love. Conditional love is when one has to earn love or gets love by doing things. Unconditional love is about loving someone for who they are. Conditional love happens in the chaotic church because the members need acceptance and approval from others. Although the church members approach each other with disregard for each other, at the same time, underneath all of that, there is a game that is played where members need to earn love. This conditional love is earned through being nice to others, giving money to the church, and stroking the church leaders with words and food. Conditional love is gained when the members restrain themselves from complaining and arguing. Just going along with whatever is happening is another way to gain love. This is spiritually abusive.

Each knows best

It's spiritually abusive when a church fails to stand on creeds and confessions and abide by them. Chaotic churches believe that each knows best what is believed and accepted as true. This causes the members of the church to lack unity and oneness because there is no common ground of belief. There is risk about who and what is right when each is deciding best in his/her heart about what the Bible teaches.

Similar to this is the approach of "if it feels good, do it." The chaotic church not only says that each decides what to believe, it also stresses that feelings can be used when determining truth. Feelings are fickle. Feelings are slippery. Feelings are not about knowledge. However, going by feelings is what chaotic churches do. Remember, chaotic churches don't stress about making sure they are on target about what they Bible teaches. They embrace the idea that each knows best.

Everyone is saved

It's "easy come, easy go" at the Community Church of Chaos. Everyone is saved so there's no need to stress about sin, repentance, or recommitting oneself to God. "It's not that hard to get into heaven" is their belief and fears about hell are snuffed out. How one lives life becomes irrelevant. God excuses homosexual lifestyle, gay marriages, and the use of open marriages. Forgiveness is quick and easy. God loves everyone. This is spiritually abusive.

No traditions

Chaotic churches do not believe in doing things the same. They are quick to use any new style of worship that is suggested because keeping to traditions is not important. Times at church are simplistic and easy when there are few guidelines about what church should be. There is no desire to establish and maintain meaningful worship. This is spiritually abusive.

No accountability

No one answers to anyone else when there is no accountability in a church system. Sin is dismissed quickly and easily, and there is no need for confession and repentance. This creates an atmosphere where sin is minimized and living life as one wants to is acceptable. It's spiritually abusive when sin happens and accountability for the one who harmed does not happen.

Fortune (1994, p. 7) in her book *Sexual Abuse by Clergy*, speaks about how when clergy have sex with others, it is exploitative and abusive. The four reasons given to support this include that is it a violation of the role of clergy, there is misuse of authority and power by the clergy, clergy is taking advantage of the vulnerable, and this is not an issue of meaningful consent. In her discussion about justice-making, she shares that one of the things that needs to happen so the victim can forgive is for the abusive clergy to be held accountable for what he did. Church does harm to its victims and members when leaders are not held accountable for what they do.

Individualism

One's name is in the membership book, but the chaotic church is not about fellowship and ties with one another. Each may think and do as they want. Each may determine what is right and good in their hearts. Each may conduct their lives and affairs as they see best. One is on their own in the chaotic church. The idea that each lives in their own bubble creates a faith life that is grounded on one's own beliefs and values.

It's more than spiritual abuse

Chaotic church leadership is more than spiritual abuse, much more. This approach of no rules or expectations leads to leaders and members doing to each other as they want. Pastors can sexually abuse members. Elders and church leaders can have sex with each other and with their members. It's okay to treat children as one wants, including sexual activity, because the church won't do anything about it anyway.

Remember, when sexual abuse happens, so do all of the rest of the abuses. So when church leaders are having sex with their congregants, sexual abuse is happening, as well as physical abuse, emotional abuse, and spiritual abuse.

How spiritually abusive churches debilitate faith in their members

The faith and life of its members are debilitated when chaos and confusion occur within the church. What the church is supposed to be, isn't. Discouragement, confusion, recklessness, and apathy set in. Carelessness, about God and the way to worship Him dominates. How leaders and members treat one another is disrespectful. Little energy is put into searching out the truth in scripture. Little focus is put into doing all the things God calls them to do. Little desire is present to obey God and follow through on His commands. Challenging one another to know the Bible is nonexistent.

Conclusion

Shame and inappropriate guilt cause harm and hurt in the chaotic church. Treatment toward one another is harsh and careless when there are poor boundaries. Appearances don't mean anything to the leaders and members. Love has to be earned. Leaders and members can decide things as they determine best in the chaotic church for they believe in the "if it feels good, do it" approach. Everyone is saved and going to heaven so there is no need to worry about getting there. God forgives easily. Traditions are not valued and there is no accountability for wrongs done by the leadership. Each conducts their lives as they see fit in their own eye.

Chapter 8
Stories of Chaotic and Spiritually Abusive Churches

The wicked bring shame and disgrace.

Pr. 13:5

1. The pastor was addicted to online gambling. As time went along, his addiction cost him more money than he had. He knew he was in trouble. So he managed to take some of the monies out of a church account when he maxed out his credit cards and his bills at home were not getting paid. When the accountant of the church realized that money was missing, he questioned what happened. The pastor came forward and admitted he took the money and that he had a gambling addiction.

    As the elders discussed what happened, they realized that everyone has problems, even pastors. So instead of insisting that the money be paid back, it was agreed that the money would be taken out of other accounts to cover the amount that was missing. Although the pastor was confronted about what happened, nothing else was done, including the elders failure to require the pastor to get help for his addiction.

It is spiritually abusive when a pastor, who represents God and His Church, misuses his money and time to fulfill his own personal needs. The elders showed that obedience to God and what scripture teaches are unimportant when issues of stewardship and stealing money from church accounts come forward.

2. The pastor was irritable and had anger issues. It was apparent to his church that his moods could be up or down or something inbetween. Over time, both the elders and church members learned that when it came to asking him something, it depended on what mood he had at that moment.

As time went along, certain congregants became aware of an alcohol smell on the pastor's breath. Soon comments were being made to the elders about the number of empty alcohol bottles and beer cans that were seen in his garage. On one occasion, when an elder stopped by the pastor's office, an open can of beer was found on his desk with others in his backpack.

Then it happened. It was at an evening service that it was obvious to the attendees that the pastor was slurring his words and was easily confused about the order of worship. When it became apparent that he could not continue, an elder came forward and directed the pastor to take a seat in the pew while the elder dismissed the congregation.

When the issues were reviewed at the next elder meeting, it was decided that the pastor would go to alcohol treatment for two weeks and then return to his normal work schedule.

It's spiritually abusive when a pastor, who represents God and His Church, drinks excessively and is drunk when leading worship. The elders' failure to deal with his drinking and behavior further defames God's name. This also is spiritually abusive.

3. The church authorities okayed gay lifestyle and same sex marriages for their members. However, certain church leaders were not satisfied that only members were allowed to do this. Then one of the church's pastors came forward and admitted to his congregation that he had a desire for same sex relationships, too. He presented a proposal to the regional leadership that would allow pastors and church leaders to engage in same sex relationships and marriages while serving in their ministry roles.

    After much discussion about the issue, the senior leaders of that denomination agreed that it was acceptable for their pastors to engage in gay lifestyle and same sex marriages.

    It's spiritually abusive when church leadership interprets scripture to meet their own emotional needs. It's also spiritually abusive when leadership live their lives in contradiction to what the Bible teaches.

4. The pastor had too much time on his hands. He had a hard-working congregation, an efficient

council, and a healthy congregation. The pastor was exceptionally organized in preparing for sermons and often he was ahead of schedule with it came to preparing agendas for meetings. Leading Bible studies came easy for him and he made sure that some of his time was spent with the young people.

When it became known to the elders that the pastor seemed to have too much time on his hands, they began to wonder what he was doing with his extra time. Then it happened. One of the elders came to the pastor's office unannounced. As the pastor quickly shut down his computer, the elder became curious about what he was doing online. That was when the pastor admitted to his pornography addiction.

The elder brought the situation to the next elder meeting. As it was discussed, it was agreed by the elders that everyone does it once in awhile and they directed the pastor to take a two week vacation to refocus on his ministry work.

It is spiritually abusive when a pastor engages in pornography and is sexually addicted to pornography while serving in a church leadership position. He misrepresents God and his behavior contradicts what the Bible teaches. The elders failed to confront and dismiss the pastor from his position. It is spiritually abusive for church leaders to enable someone who has deep-rooted issues to continue in a ministry role.

5. He belonged to a boys' club of his church. After going for a couple of years, he remembers telling his mom he didn't want to go anymore. He wasn't sure why; he just didn't want to.

As he came to his adult years, he realized that he struggled with anxiety and depression. He was in and out of therapy, but he never was able to tap into why he lacked energy and focus for his day to day activities.

After losing his employment and his marriage, he moved into the basement of his mom's house. While attending a support group, it occurred to him. He asked the leader, "If someone was abused as a child, would that still affect the person as an adult?" The answer was yes. He was beginning to understand why he was the way he was.

In his search for what happened at the church of his childhood, he discovered that he along with several other young boys was sexually abused by the one of the club leaders. The leader would take the boys on camping trips and often during those times, the leader sexually molested and fondled the boys. He was one of them.

His memory of those years started to surface. The parents of one of the boys reported the abuse to the elders of the church. He remembered how the boys were told at an evening church service that they were to "forgive and move on" in regard to what the leader did. It was found that the parents of the boys were never informed about what happened, there was no call in to child protection services, and none of the boys were asked if it happened to them. Nothing more was done.

It is spiritually abusive when the elders fail to investigate and confront a church leader who sexually abuses children. This is a misrepresentation of God and of His Church, and leaves children to grow up with confused and distorted thoughts and feelings of who they are and what faith in God is about.

6. It was a Sunday morning when the praise singers began to lead the worship time. Two of them were new to the team and it was obvious that the service was going to be more about a show than about worship. With a very loud band, it started out with lots of movement from the singers and the congregation was unsure how to sing the songs or what the words were. Although the lyrics were printed on the screen in the front, it was difficult to sing with the praise team leaders.

This went on for some time. Then the pastor of the church came forward and announced that since the rhythm was catchy and a break was needed from the usual format of worship, he gave permission to the praise team to continue.

After about an hour, the pastor read a small piece of scripture. Then the praise team returned and did a skit about the ten commandments. It all ended in laughter and comments from the congregation were about how much fun church was and how they needed more worship times like this one.

It is spiritually abusive for congregations to be in the presence of God for worship that is more about entertainment than anything else. Persons attending this event come to believe that irreverence for God is okay and worship is about a good time and fun. Church leaders who are allowing this are misrepresenting God which is spiritually abusive.

PART III
HEALTHY CHURCH LEADERSHIP

Chapter 9
At the Healthy, Spiritually Rich Church

You, be strong in the grace that is in Christ Jesus.
2 Tim. 2:1

Faye began by sharing that she came to therapy to discuss events that happened at an overnight church event. She told her therapist that she always enjoyed the church she and her family went to and now as a teen, she was becoming more involved in their activities.

Faye told that she belonged to the youth group of the church. A yearly event of the youth group was for all of the teens of the youth group to do an overnight at the church. With two adults and the pastor sponsoring the event, parents believed it was appropriately supervised. Parents were required to sign a document that stated that they were okay with their child attending this event along with a list of rules and expectations to be followed. Included in the document was the understanding that should their child break any of the rules, the parents would be called immediately to pick up their child.

As she proceeded to tell her story, she mentioned how the games and activities that night were fun. She told how she met some new people and how a friend of hers liked a young man she met. She told that as the evening went on and it became late, it seemed that most of the youth were heading to bed. With the guys on one side of the basement and gals on the other, she told that everything seemed safe and appropriate.

Later, after she had fallen asleep in one of the back rooms, her friend woke her up. The friend explained that the new boy she met touched her inappropriately and she didn't know what to do. As she listened to what happened, Faye realized that the pastor and the sponsors needed to know what happened.

They reported to the adults about what happened. The pastor immediately found the young man, asked him about what happened, and called his parents. When the parents arrived to pick him up, the pastor explained to the parents what happened. The pastor also told the parents that this was a mandated reporting incident and he would be contacting the police in the morning.

From there, the friend said she felt okay with staying the remainder of the night with the understanding that the adults would explain things to her parents in the morning. When morning came, the pastor told the parents what happened and that the police would be called. Upon the arrival of the police, the girl shared with the officer what happened. He asked that she come to the police station, along with her parents, the pastor, and the adults, to write a report. They agreed.

Now it was several weeks since the reporting. Faye shared that she was directed by the detective to begin counseling. Faye stated that the church as willing to pay for some of the counseling services. Also the pastor and sponsors kept in contact with her to make sure she was doing okay. The accused was taken into custody for questioning and was to appear in court in a few days.

The detective in the case commended the pastor for reporting this incident to the police. He stated that the perpetrator had previous charges and he showed a history of molesting young girls.

The church leaders did several things right in sponsoring this overnight church event. They required the parents of the youth to sign a document that stated the rules and expectations for the event. Consequences for inappropriate behavior by the youth were explained in the document. When the mandated reporting incident happened, there was no hesitation on the part of the pastor to call the police in the morning. He could have called it in immediately, but mandating report can wait for 24 hours if the victim is not in immediate danger. With the young man sent home and the victim safe, it was appropriate to wait till morning. This also allowed the parents to be informed about what happened prior to involving the police.

It was appropriate for the church to offer monies for the counseling services and Faye shared that the church leaders decided that the accused is banned from anymore church activities. The pastor and church leaders checked in with her from time to time to ensure that she was doing okay.

Chapter 10
Healthy and Spiritually Rich Churches

Live lives worthy of God.

1 Thess. 2:12

What is a healthy and spiritually rich church?

A healthy and spiritually rich church is a place where people come together to meet and worship God. This faith community provides opportunities for members and visitors to grow in the knowledge and grace of their heavenly Father.

What does a healthy and spiritually rich church look like?

A healthy and spiritually rich church is a church that gives honor and glory to God through all they do.

Worship at a healthy church is orderly and respectful. Their worship contains times for prayer, singing, Bible reading, giving to needy causes, and the preaching of God's Word. For some churches, there is time for personal testimonies. The worship times are both a time for praising God and a time for quiet reflection on God. Worship is not about entertainment or show, but rather about thanksgiving and honor to God.

A healthy church is a safe church. The leadership and members show respect for one another, welcome visitors and new attendees into church activities, and accept one another for where they are in their faith walk with God. They ensure that their children and youth programs are safe from predators and abusers. They allow open communication from anyone who has concerns about church events or activities.

A healthy church knows how to flex and bend. This means that the leadership is willing to make changes that could enhance worship and spiritual growth in faith and life. Leadership recognizes manipulation and control by fellow leaders or members and is quick to stop harmful behaviors by anyone in the church.

Care and concern for members and attendees are a part of a healthy church. They pray for each other, provide emotional support and encouragement to one another, and build each other up in the Lord. Leaders and members do not engage in gossip and slander, defamation, or are party to causing harm to families or relationships.

Serving one another and the community are priorities in the healthy church. They put the needs of others before their own and give up time and use their talents to bring honor to God. Their desire is to renew and revive the spiritual lives of their people. They use healthy boundaries to prevent enabling or intrusive behaviors from occurring and are assertive when they need to be.

This striving for a church not to be rigid or chaotic can be seen as a church whose leaders know how to balance rational and emotional thinking. Rational thinking is when emotion is not a part of discussing the issue whereas emotional thinking is addressing an issue that is drenched in emotion. Richardson

(1996) speaks about the higher the differentiation there is for a person, the healthier the person is. The four levels are

1. the ability to perceive more accurately the reality of situations, to not create threat that really isn't there, and to discern what is actually threatening and how;
2. the ability to identify his or her own opinions, beliefs, values, and commitments, and the principles of behavior that derive from these, as they are relevant to a particular situation;
3. the ability to think clearly and wisely about possible options for action and are likely consequences for each of these option; and
4. the ability to act flexibly within the situation on the basis of these perceptions, thoughts and principles (p. 86).

This can also be said for churches and church leaders.

Healthy church leaders spiritually enhance their members

Healthy church leaders are transparent and humble. They are willing to try new things when they know it's crucial for spiritual growth of their members. They are not easily threatened by change and do not become anxious when problems arise. They trust that God will help them through the difficult times.

Healthy church leaders know their weaknesses and strengths. They recognize within themselves when they need to use their talents and gifts for the church and when they need to let others step in and help. Their accomplishments and successes are not about how great or smart they are, for they refuse to allow pride or arrogance to enter in. They are quick to thank God for when they could serve and help others. They have inner confidence,

addresses such issues in the prayerful hopes that worship and interactions with one another can be changed so that meaningful worship and interactions with one another can continue. The healthy church recognizes that some traditions can become god-like in that people come to believe that traditions are a part of one's salvation. This is idolatry and becomes adulterous.

Examples of keeping good traditions include how the Lord's Supper is done as Christ commanded in the New Testament, that believers do not give up meeting together, and that the confessions of sin and the promise of forgiveness are both taught in the Bible.

Accountability

In the healthy and spiritually rich church, the strength of membership is that there is accountability to one another and to leadership. Answering to leadership is important because it keeps members in tune with living their lives in ways that honor God. Should members stray from what scripture teaches, the leaders and members can challenge the person to reevaluate what they are thinking and doing in hopes to bring them back to what the Bible says. This redirection from leaders and members is done with care and love.

Along with this, leaders and members know that when they are holding another accountable, that they are addressing the wrong a person has done, not the person themselves. Healthy churches recognize that personal attacks on others do not bring change. Overcorrecting and controlling others brings forth resistance and rebellion. Firm warnings and biblically based correction, entrenched with prayer, are done with hope of change.

Serve others, not serve self

The healthy church does not look at their congregants and expect them to serve their leaders; rather the leaders ask how they can best serve their members. Also, the healthy church leaders and members look at how they can best serve others and their community, rather than what the church can do for them. The healthy church embraces opportunities to bring healing and ministry and does it in a way that maintains healthy boundaries and expectations for those they serve. This is done in the spirit of love and grace.

Conclusion

The spirit-rich church does not shame and guilt each another or those of their community. They show respect for each other by using healthy boundaries and they love each other unconditionally. They know that God knows best in all situations and they turn to Him when problems and crises arise. Salvation is by grace alone and they know how to use a balance of knowledge, emotion, and response to address issues. Traditions are maintained only when they are edifying and beneficial for worship and members, and accountability of leadership to members and members to members is the strength of creating a healthy church. The work of the church is about serving others whether it's fellow members or others of their faith community.

Chapter 11
The Effects of Healthy and Spiritually Rich Churches

The mind controlled by the Spirit is life and peace.

Rom. 8:6

Humility and transparency

The healthy and spiritually rich church is humble and transparent. They know who they are and are well established in doctrine and in life. Their identity is found in Jesus Christ and His teachings. Their focus is about honoring and glorifying God and they know their mission is to reconcile the world through Christ.

They often accomplish much in their work because of this. God blesses them, through good times and bad. Their successes do not lead to pride or arrogance, and they acknowledge that God is the One who empowers them to do more than they ever thought they could do.

Transparency is allowing others to see one's true self without being defensive or reactive. This true self is about one's self-confidence, founded in knowing who one is and accepting faults and short-comings as reality. There are no cover-ups or pretending. There is no fakeness or façade. Embracing who one really is, is the strength of a healthy person.

For the healthy church, it's the same. Leaders and members know that they are not perfect nor would pretend to be. They recognize faults and short-comings. They are saddened by their mistakes and take their sins seriously. They are not arrogant, self-righteous, or chaotic. They refuse to be manipulated.

Leaders take their role as leader in the church to heart. They diligently strive to please God in their calling as church leader and use wise and discerning counsel for those God places in their care. They are effective communicators, are good role models, and demonstrate what it means to be a healthy church leader and member.

How healthy and spiritually rich leadership affects church members

Church members are watching their church leaders. Church members want to model after their leaders.

They recognize that church leaders are not easily manipulated. They respect how their leaders use appropriate boundaries with them and others. They experience unconditional love from their leaders and trust develops with them. They learn that each person is a vital part of the membership and that respect leads to a desire to strive harder in their Christian walk. Accountability helps leaders and members to do a self-check, which leads to members doing a reevaluation of their faith and life, to ensure they are doing all they can to please and honor God. There is flexibility in the relationships to each other. Dictatorship and unhealthy control are not used. Members do not feel heaviness and badness, but rather a joy that they are a forgiven people and are deeply loved by their heavenly Father. They understand that they need to work together, use a give and take approach, and accept one another's faults without judging.

Members model humbleness and transparency which they learn from their leaders. They show love and grace to those around them. Their motives do not come from wanting to be noticed or recognized, and it's not because they want acceptance and approval from others. Instead, because their love for God overflows in their hearts, they want to share that love with others.

They

- affirm and encourage;
- use healthy boundaries;
- have unconditional love;
- are obedient to scripture;
- respond out of thanksgiving;
- help their members to grow spiritually;
- understand and balance emotion;
- know how to flex and bend;
- use accountability; and
- use and model servant hood.

Let's look more closely at the healthy church.

Affirming and encouraging

Healthy churches affirm and encourage one another. With their words and actions, they do as best they can to bring good to their people and others, in the hopes that as life becomes hard and difficult, getting through it is possible. This assures people that they are never alone in their trials and that God comes to them through his Spirit and through the touch and words of His people.

Healthy boundaries

Some people understand church as a place where they do things for others for free. It's thought of as a place to get money and free things. This is prevented by using healthy boundaries. They know when to say no to people and they know when to flex and bend in dealing with others. They develop and use policies and procedures when dealing with difficult situations so that all parties involved are protected.

Their approach to healthy boundaries teaches leaders and members to respect each other. They do not feel guilt or shame when they use appropriate boundaries, but instead feel empowered that they are doing what they need to do to keep all people safe. Healthy boundaries prevent recklessness and sloppiness in the governance of the church.

Unconditional love

Unconditional love draws people to the healthy church. Because there is no judging, gossip, or slander when unconditional love is present, trust for the church and its members develops. When trust grows at the healthy church, honesty and truthfulness in the hearts of the people grows. This growth causes transparency and acceptance of self and others and leaders and members become more honest with God. When Christians are honest with God, they understand God and their faith better. Faith becomes stronger. And love for each other deepens.

Obedience to scripture

Spiritually rich churches obey God. They take His laws and commands seriously. They obey the teachings in the Bible and they strive to implement what they learn from the Bible into their lives.

They know that love for God is shown by their obedience to Him. However, they also know that this does not mean they may control and dictate to others about how they are to live and what they are to do and not do. They realize they have a plank in their own eyes. They take their desire to obey scripture along with their calling as a church leader and member, and discern, with God's help, in how to deal with others.

Response of thanksgiving

Healthy church leaders and members know it's all about God. They know that all the things they do are always done with God's help. Salvation is free. It is God's gift to them. Their response is one of thanksgiving to God. This thanksgiving is shown by ministering to the sick and poor, helping those who are distressed and hurting, and sharing with those in need. This giving is not done for show or recognition and it is not done for praise or attention. It is done out of a response for what God did for them.

Spiritually growing

The healthy church's desire is for all members and others to grow when they attend and belong to their church. Their goal is that the knowledge and understanding of God may increase in the hearts of their people and that the church does all it can to make that happen. The healthy church is open to new worshipping approaches if it's believed that spiritual growth would be enhanced. The healthy church is willing to change traditions and routines if the older way to doing it is no longer meaningful. New ways to do things, including new worship styles and new Bible studies, are encouraged if it doesn't contradict what the Bible teaches.

The healthy church approaches change with care. They do not become reckless with the idea of change. They weigh the change carefully, making sure that the change is honoring to God, and that the change would be spiritually enhancing for their people.

Understanding emotion

God made people with emotions. Emotions are the feelings people have as life is experienced. In many unhealthy churches, emotions are not managed well. In the rigid church, emotions are ignored and denied. In chaotic churches, decisions and actions are made on emotion. Both are not good.

Emotion, in the healthy church, is where God is experienced. Emotion is what leaders and members have when death or illness comes to the family, when someone betrays or abuses another, or when injustices occur. Emotions are slippery. They can change easily and unpredictably. That means they can't always be trusted. Sometimes, when someone says or does something that seems hurtful, time may be needed to process the feelings one has about that event.

Healthy churches know about emotions and how they can be fickle. They know that it is important to lead the church with the proper balance of emotion versus rational thinking. When there is the proper blend of both, good decisions are made. Leaders and members need time to think about what to do in order to make sound, logical decisions. Healthy churches know that and do that.

Richardson (1996, p. 51) speaks about the importance of leaders keeping calm when crises arise in the church. This is primarily done by individuals, whether leaders or not, who focus on managing their own emotions when issues surface. They do not tell people to be calm, but instead bring calmness to the people through their demeanor and responses. While keeping control of their own emotion, they also connect themselves with those who are anxious. This helps bring healthy responses to issues in the church.

Flex and bend

Rigid church leaders are harsh and strict in their approach to leadership. Chaotic churches use the "it doesn't really matter" attitude in their leadership approach. Healthy churches are neither.

Healthy churches know the importance of how to flex and bend. This means they do not control other people, dictate to others how things are suppose to be done, or use shame and blame when things don't go their way. Flex and bend for the healthy church means they are willing to hear other points of view and perspectives. They believe that traditions do not have to be continued because it's always been done that way.

Healthy churches are open to change. Leaders are okay with feedback from their members about how things are going. They desire good communication between the leaders and their members.

Accountability

Accountability is something rigid and chaotic churches become confused about. The rigid church thinks that accountability is how they control members. The chaotic church says that there is no such thing as accountability. The healthy church doesn't support either of these.

Accountability is a part of having membership at a church. Accountability is answering to someone. At work, a person is accountable to the manager or the supervisor. At church, members are accountable to the leadership of the church and to one another.

Healthy churches use accountability. When the faith and life of a member is straying, he/she is answerable to the church. This means that the church can confront and address the wrongs they see the member doing and the member needs to give an account to what is happening. The goal of the confrontation between the leader and the member is to help the member to change and to come to a better place in his/her faith and life. The leader also learns about the struggles the member is going through.

But it works the other way, too, for no one lives in isolation from one another in the church. Members hold leaders and other members accountable. Members can bring grievances against a leader through a church process and members can hold other members accountable by using Matthew 18.

Human nature wants to rebel against accountability. This is all the more reason why accountability at church is important. In the healthy church, leaders hold other leaders and members accountable and members hold leaders and other members accountable.

Servant-hood

Servant-hood is something that is easy to say, hard to do. People resist serving others because it is about giving to others with little or no return. Servant-hood can be about feeling unappreciated when good is given to another and the temptation to resent it is there.

Healthy and spiritually rich churches are servants. They believe that they are here to serve others without grumbling or complaining. They do work for others out of a heart of love and support and enjoy opportunities to give back to God's broken world.

Servant-hood in the healthy church keeps no records of wrongs. It does not keep score of who did more than another and healthy servants resist the temptation of passive aggressive remarks. Servant-hood bends the knee to others.

Conclusion

The effects of the healthy church are many. Healthy and spiritually rich churches encourage and affirm one another. They use healthy boundaries and embrace one another with unconditional love. They strive to obey scripture in all things and they do good to others out of a heart of thanksgiving to God. The healthy church's desire is to enhance the spiritual growth of its members and to stress the importance of balancing emotion and rational thinking when addressing issues. Flexing and bending when needed is okay for the healthy church and they believe that holding each other accountable is what keeps leaders and members on track in their faith walk with God. Serving others brings healing and restoration to His broken world.

Chapter 12
Stories of Healthy and
Spiritually Rich Churches

A wise heart is called discerning and pleasant words promote instruction.

Prov. 16:21

1. Some of the church members desired a different style of worship. They wanted something more contemporary and less of the service lead by the pastor and more by a praise team. As ideas began to be discussed, it was apparent that there were two views on the subject with the elders knowing they were in the middle of it.

    At elders' meetings, the subject was discussed several times. They allowed some of the members who wanted to see a change to come to a meeting. The members shared their points of view, backed it up with things they had learned about what other churches were doing, and shared their own experiences regarding contemporary worship.

Then the elders listened to the side who preferred more of a traditional worship service. After some time, each of the elders agreed they needed to do their own study of this subject, ask other churches how contemporary worship was working, and visit a few churches they knew who were using it. It was agreed that each would report about what they discovered in two months.

When the discussion time occurred, each brought his/her ideas to the table. After discussing it again, it was decided that they would proceed with a gradual change to contemporary worship, with each of the steps spelled out by the pastor. The pastor along with two elders would work to finding a worship leader who would eventually put together a worship committee. This committee would report to the elders at each elders' meeting.

The elders also decided that they would send out a memo to the members, sharing what they decided to try, and a note of encouragement would be included for the members to be open to change.

It was agreed that after three months the elders would allow feedback through a survey to provide opportunity to express how members felt about the changes. The elders also encouraged all members to speak with them about any concerns.

The church leadership was healthy by being open to doing a change in worship, researching the topic themselves, and discussing this issue with themselves and others. Although they knew there would be some resistance to change, they were open to do it gradually, with check-in to make sure it was going okay, and with time and opportunity for members to express their thoughts and feelings.

2. The pastor was skilled at manipulating his elders. From years of working in ministry, he learned that most churches adore their pastor. He also learned that once he is in a church for awhile, he can con the elders into doing almost anything.

He was still somewhat new to the congregation. Although he didn't have the elders exactly figure out, he was growing in confidence that again, he would be able to manipulate the elders into doing things.

First it was small things. He tried to get them to change the hymnal the church was using. He explained how the book had a few songs in it that were in contradiction to the teachings of the church. He said he wanted the books out of the pews and to order different ones. The elders were surprised by this issue, but then agreed that they would talk about it within the next year.

Then the pastor wanted something changed in his salary. He explained that if certain things were done differently, he would be able to save money on taxes. The elders were not so easily convinced it was legal and said they would have to talk to their tax person to check into this. They would look into it within the next few months.

More and more issues came forward as time went along. And the elders learned more and more that what they needed to say was no to the pastor's requests. They also began to see a pattern of behavior that was a concern to them.

Then it happened. All along the secretary of the church was communicating to the elders that the pastor was trying to change things that she didn't think should be changed. When she finally became weary of dealing with his insistence about what she was to do, she told him no. He became angry and threw a book at her. The book missed her, broke a window behind her, while he stomped out of the building.

She called the police.

Then she called the president of the elders and told him what was happening. He managed to come right away. She reported to the police what happened, stated that she was unsure where he went, and that she was fearful about what he would do if he would return.

The police officer and the elder talked things out and they managed to reach the pastor on his cell phone. He was asked to return to the church because the officer wanted to speak with him. He came.

At the next elders meeting, it was decided that the pastor was on a month leave of absence, which would give the elders time to determine how to proceed with the pastor. A month later, he was dismissed from serving in that church.

This church was healthy in many ways. The secretary followed the safety policy that the church established several years prior. That church reviewed safety polices every year which enabled the secretary to know what she was to do in that situation. Second, the elders did not necessarily meet every request the pastor had. They used good boundaries by saying they would think about it or by saying no. The elders and the secretary were not easily controlled by his anger. When the pastor got angry, they did what they knew needed to be done and were not intimidated by him.

3. The pastor had a way of popping in on people at their homes during the day. He seemed especially to like doing this to women whose husbands were gone to work. If women stopped by church to drop something off, he was quick to step away from his desk and visit with them. He often mentioned to them that should they ever need time to talk, his office was open to do so. He has flexible hours. The women were enjoying the attention.

As time went by, some of the women began to think differently about this. They shared with each other what the pastor was doing and expressed concern that this was not healthy behavior on the part of the pastor. One wondered if some of this was about flirting and another described it as "crossing the line." They agreed with each other that there needed to be at least one other person around when the pastor would stop by their house and that they needed to say no to him more often.

Then it happened. One of the women came forward and told the elders about inappropriate touch by the pastor. She explained to them what happened in the church kitchen when she was preparing food for a church supper and asked them what she should do. They immediately directed her to the grievance policy of the church which was used for such instances. They encouraged her to submit it as soon as she could.

She did.

Within days, the elders held an immediate meeting to discuss how to proceed. It was agreed that two of them would meet with the woman, along with her support person, to give her opportunity to speak about the issue. She agreed to come in.

Next the two elders reported back to the full elder board about what she said. They agreed that the next step was to speak to the pastor and hear his side of things. They communicated this to the woman. Two of them met with the pastor and after hearing his side of things, reported to the full elder board that the pastor needs to meet with the full elder board.

Within days, the full elder board met with the pastor. He was questioned by the elder board and seemed honest in his admittance of what he did. He showed some remorse.

After deliberations, it was agreed that the congregation would need to know some of what happened, while limiting information to protect the woman. An announcement took place and a letter with similar information was sent to each member.

The pastor was put on paid leave and after several months, was removed from that church. Regional pastors were given the responsibility to address what the future would be for the pastor.

The healthy church did several things right. They had a grievance policy in place and were able to direct the complainant to it so that she could present her concerns in a document. The elders took the matter seriously, met with each other and the involved parties immediately, and took action. It was appropriate in how they communicated to the church about what happened, gave protection to the victim, and understood that the pastor had to be dismissed because of safety issues for the members.

4. It seemed that it was all about him. At first, the pastor's charm was a big attraction to his new congregation. He was able to engage with about every member, was able to lead Bible studies with charm and wit, and after church was the kind of person everyone wanted to talk to.

    The elders also bought into his charm, at least at first. They found him engaging, knowledgeable about church business, and quite outspoken. To some extent this was a relief for them, because morale was low at elders' meetings for some time.

    After time passed and the new pastor settled in, the elders began to notice some things. One thing was how the pastor seemed to have extra time on his hands. They were hearing reports about how the wasn't at the office that much, that he was hard to get a hold of during the day, and that he was busy with a new hobby he had, horses.

    When the leadership confronted him about office hours and where he was spending his time, he shared that he moved his church computer to his home office. He stated that he liked to work from home because it was easier. The elders reported to him that people were having some trouble reaching him and that he needed to get a cell phone if he wanted to have his office from home. He agreed.

Things did not improve with these changes. People continued to complain about not being able to reach him. They told that they left messages on his cell phone, but he never returned their calls.

Then it happened to an elder. He tried to reach the pastor's cell phone, but he didn't answer. The elder left a message. When the pastor did not return his call within one day, the elder stopped by the pastor's home to see if he was around. He was not there.

A few hours later the elder called the pastor again. The pastor answered. The elder asked why he hadn't returned his call. The pastor went into an explanation about being busy, that he couldn't be interrupted while studying a sermon, and he had a sick child who he had to take care of.

The elder was confused. He told that pastor that he was going to stop by the office and speak with him. When the elder did, he confronted the pastor again about why he didn't return the phone call and that he (the elder) had stopped by at the home office but no one was there. He asked for an explanation.

When the pastor's answer seemed vague and conflicting, the elder decided to wait with his response and report what happened to the lead of the elder board. He did.

Three of the elders, including the one who reported the incident, ask to meet with the pastor. In this meeting, they questioned again where the pastor was when the elder was looking for him, explaining that the details of this situation were not making sense, and reminding him they needed the truth.

The pastor, realizing that he needed to be truthful, told the whole story of the day. It came out that he was addicted to porn. He told how he was at a porn magazine store that day, that he was addicted to online pornography, and that he was meeting with others to sexually act out. As he told his history, it became apparent that he had been addicted to porn since his college years, that he tried many times to quit, and that he knew it was wrong, but couldn't stop himself.

The three elders documented the pastor's admittance carefully. They told him that this would be reported to the elders and they would have an emergency meeting within the next few days about what he said. He was suspended from preaching, effective immediately, and stated that the church computer would be confiscated immediately. He was told that the elders would be calling him after the elders decide how to proceed with things. He understood.

The pastor never returned to the pulpit. Under the care and direction of the elders, he was sent to sexual addiction treatment, was to participate in therapy treatment, and eventually was dismissed from ministry.

The healthy church did several things right. They took the complaints about the members not being able to reach the pastor seriously. They confronted the pastor when the complaints continued. When one of the elders experienced the same problems that the members were talking about, the elder investigated. Action taken by the elders was immediate and the removal from office showed that they took a stand against pornography and sexual addiction. By sending the pastor to treatment and dismissing him from ministry, they were being the most loving they could be. It showed that they cared for their fallen brother.

5. She managed to get herself on committees that gave her the most attention. Going from one committee to another, she soon convinced the leadership that she should be on the worship committee. They agreed to let her join.

    As the meeting began, she knew that this was the right committee for her. She began to enjoy the attention that comes with leading the praise team and worship committee. She began to research all kinds of songs and texts that could be used in worship. She had opportunity to meet with the pastor and get to know him on a more personal level. She enjoyed meeting new people and trying new things for the church. She was convinced it was a fit for her.

    As time went along, some of the committee members were having concerns about the woman. They noticed how she dominated the meetings, was insistent that thing be done her way, and it was apparent that she liked to be standing in front during worship services. It seemed that she was being more of an entertainer than a worship leader.

Then it happened. While leading a worship service, she privied herself to tell a personal story of her own. Without permission from the leadership team or the elders, she went into a story of her childhood. Some of the details of her story were not appropriate for worship and eventually, as she ended what she wanted to say, she was in tears. With awkward moments, everyone fell silent. Finally, the other worship leader took the lead and the congregation sang a song.

Later, in review of what happened, she was confronted about what she did. Having only recently reviewed the expectations about how to be a worship leader, the committee decided that she was no longer to serve in this capacity.

As she became angry about their decision, the worship team involved the pastor and the elders to help. After meeting with them, it was agreed that she needed to address the childhood issues she talked about and she would no longer be involved in the worship leadership team.

The healthy church did several things right. They had a review of what it meant to be in the role of a worship leader. This document was reviewed from time to time. Second, when she went against what she was suppose to do, she was dismissed. When she became angry, the pastor and the elders were involved to address the issue. Directing her to get some counseling was appropriate.

6. He pounded his fist on the elders' table. This elder was angry because things were not going his way. He wanted the pastor out of their church and the other

elders were saying there were not enough grounds or evidence that would support that decision.

When he didn't get his way, he obsessed about every little thing the pastor did. He criticized his sermons, he checked to see if announcements were right on the bulletin, he stopped by the church to see how often the pastor was in his office, and he called people to see if the pastor was at meetings he was suppose to be at.

At one point, the elder became so obsessed about getting the pastor out, he began to gossip and slander the pastor's wife. He told lies about her and said that she wasn't fit to serve on committees. He described her as depressed and that she should be getting counseling. He told about how she was an unfit mother.

Finally, when the congregants realized what the elder was doing, some of them joined together to write a letter to the lead of elders. It was asked in that letter that confidentiality be honored and that those writing the letter not be revealed. In that letter, which was written with respect for all parties involved, they stated what the elder was saying about the pastor and his wife. They asked for a meeting with the elders.

The elders agreed to meet with the individuals. Throughout that meeting, it became apparent that the elder would be confronted about the issue.

Later, the three elders met with the elder. They explained what they were told about him. After admitting that he was doing some of what he was being accused of, it was agreed that the elder was under censorship and until things were resolved, was limited in his role as elder. For the pastor and his wife, the elders spoke with both together, asking them if they were aware that this happened, and how they could help them through this time.

The healthy church was appropriate to meet with the concerned members, to confront the elder, and to restrict him in his role as elder. It was good that the elders also met with both the pastor and his wife to encourage them and ask them about how they could help. The elders were not manipulated by the elder's anger and instead, were able to confront him on his wrongdoing.

CONCLUSION

Chapter 13
Determining Your Church's
Leadership Style

Love does no harm.

Romans 13:10

We have walked through a discussion of two extreme church leadership styles and explored a third. If we were to draw out what this book describes on a continuum, it may look something like this:

Rigid   Healthy   Chaotic

X_____ X_____X

Think carefully about how your pastor and church leaders lead your church. Individually, some may seem rigid and controlling while others approach leadership as it doesn't really matter what happens.

As best you can, place the pastor and each elder on the line above. Give reasons that support why you put each person in the place you put them. Collectively, ask if you think the leadership is heavy on one end or the other. If many are found on the rigid end, know that your church approaches leadership with many rules and narrow expectations, and they use defensiveness and reactivity when others challenge them. They are anxious in their approach to leading and fear any time their members sin and violate one of the laws.

If many of your leaders land on the chaotic end, then your church uses a permissive approach to leadership. They believe in few rules or guidelines, make decisions based on the thought for the moment, and have identity and purpose issues. They are okay with having sex with each other, don't want to hold people accountable to the leadership of the church or to one other, and they prefer to blend in with the culture around them than to stand for a biblical principle.

Conclusion

The goal in effective and healthy church leadership is to use moderation. It's healthy to be in the middle of the continuum. Rules, expectations, accountability, and a show of responsibility are all needed, but with balance. Bending and flexing are necessary, believing that God is merciful and just needs to be embraced, and assuring that leadership represents who God is about is paramount.

Spiritual abuse happens when there is heaviness on either side of the continuum. Spiritually rich churches are the ones that do things in moderation, hold each other accountable to using a balanced approach, stay within biblical boundaries when leading, and strive in every way to do what pleases God.

References

Fortune, Marie M. *Love Does No Harm*, New York: Continuum, 1995.

Fortune, Marie M., and James N. Poling. *Sexual Abuse by Clergy: A Crisis for the Church,* Dacatur: Journal of Pastoral Care Publications, Inc., 1996.

Laaser, Mark. *Healing the Wounds of Sexual Addiction*, Grand Rapids: Zondervan, 2004.

Richardson, Ronald W. *Creating a Healthier Church*, Minneapolis: Fortress Press, 1996.

VanVonderen, Jeff. *Tired of Trying to Measure Up*, Minneapolis: Bethany House Publishers, 1989.